CHRISTMAS PLANNER

SIMPLE, CUTE, CHRISTMAS ORGANIZER, HOLIDAY TIPS, WISHLIST, BUCKET LIST, MONTHLY CALENDAR, WEEKLY PLANNER, DAILY PLANNER, TO-DO LIST, BUDGET TRACKER, CHRISTMAS CARD TRACK

SNEHA AMIN

AF406136

Copyright © Sneha Amin
All Rights Reserved.

This book has been self-published with all reasonable efforts taken to make the material error-free by the author. No part of this book shall be used, reproduced in any manner whatsoever without written permission from the author, except in the case of brief quotations embodied in critical articles and reviews.

The Author of this book is solely responsible and liable for its content including but not limited to the views, representations, descriptions, statements, information, opinions and references ["Content"]. The Content of this book shall not constitute or be construed or deemed to reflect the opinion or expression of the Publisher or Editor. Neither the Publisher nor Editor endorse or approve the Content of this book or guarantee the reliability, accuracy or completeness of the Content published herein and do not make any representations or warranties of any kind, express or implied, including but not limited to the implied warranties of merchantability, fitness for a particular purpose. The Publisher and Editor shall not be liable whatsoever for any errors, omissions, whether such errors or omissions result from negligence, accident, or any other cause or claims for loss or damages of any kind, including without limitation, indirect or consequential loss or damage arising out of use, inability to use, or about the reliability, accuracy or sufficiency of the information contained in this book.

Made with ♥ on the Notion Press Platform
www.notionpress.com

1

Table of Content

Wish List
Bucket List
Weekly Planner
Day Planner
To Do List
Get Shopping List
Expense Tracker
Christmas Card Tracker
Favourite Recipes
Chirtmas Memories
Note For Next Year

2

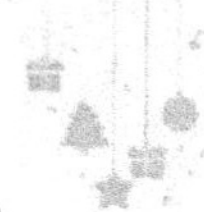

My Christmas Wishlist

These are few of my favorite things

My Christmas Wishlist

These are few of my favorite things

My Christmas Wishlist
These are few of my favorite things

5

My Christmas Wishlist
These are few of my favorite things

My Christmas Wishlist

These are few of my favorite things

My Christmas Wishlist
These are few of my favorite things

My Christmas Wishlist
These are few of my favorite things

My Christmas Wishlist

These are few of my favorite things

My Christmas Wishlist

These are few of my favorite things

11

My Christmas Wishlist

These are few of my favorite things

My Christmas Bucketlist

Fill this box with things you wish todo this Christmas Season

My Christmas Bucketlist

Fill this box with things you wish todo this Chirstmas Season

My Christmas Bucketlist
Fill this box with things you wish todo this Christmas Season

My Christmas Bucketlist

Fill this box with things you wish todo this Christmas Season

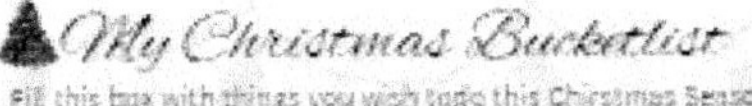

My Christmas Bucketlist

Fill this box with things you wish todo this Christmas Season

My Christmas Bucketlist

Fill this box with things you wish todo this Christmas Season

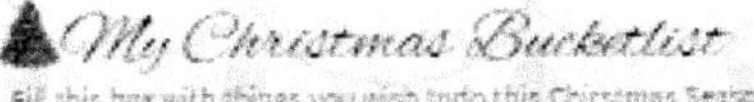

My Christmas Bucketlist

Fill this box with things you wish todo this Christmas Season

My Christmas Bucketlist

Fill this box with things you wish todo this Christmas Season

My Christmas Bucketlist

Fill this box with things you wish todo this Christmas Season

21

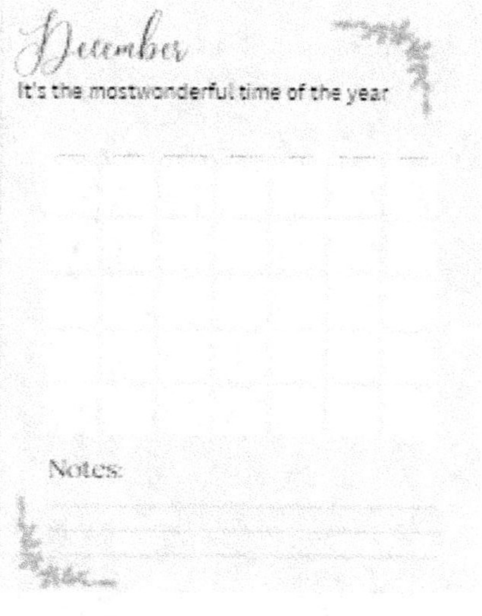

December
It's the mostwonderful time of the year
Notes:

December

It's the most wonderful time of the year

Notes:

December

It's the mostwonderful time of the year

Notes:

December

It's the mostwonderful time of the year

Notes:

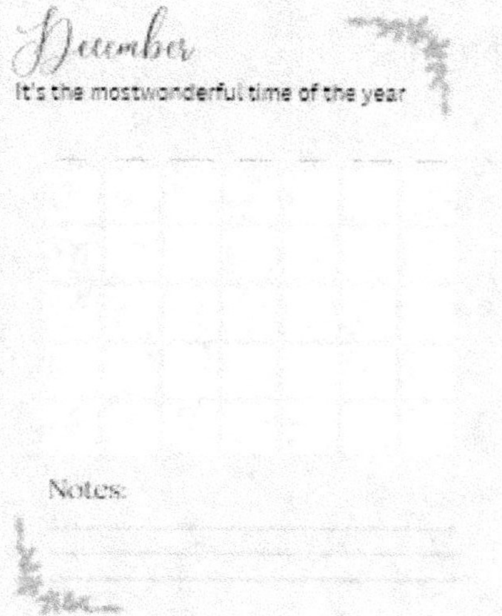

December
It's the mostwonderful time of the year
Notes:

December

It's the most wonderful time of the year

Notes:

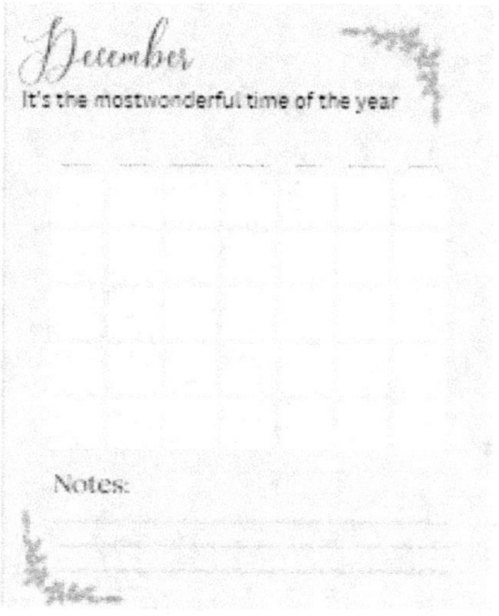

December
It's the mostwonderful time of the year
Notes:

December

It's the mostwonderful time of the year

Notes:

December

It's the most wonderful time of the year

Notes:

December

It's the most wonderful time of the year

Notes:

Weekly
Planner
"It's a good week to have
a good week"

Weekly Planner
Week Of
Month:
Week :
Sunday
Monday
Tuesday
Wednesday
Thursday
Friday
Saturday
NOTE

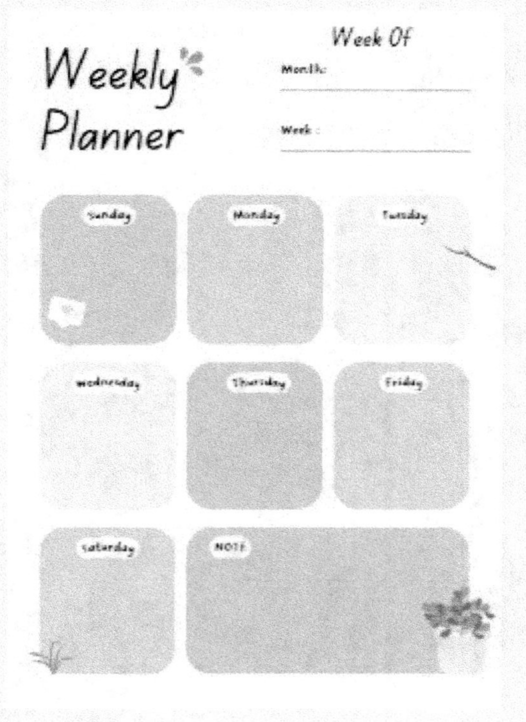

Weekly Planner
Week Of
Month:
Week :
Sunday
Monday
Tuesday
Wednesday
Thursday
Friday
Saturday
NOTE

Weekly Planner

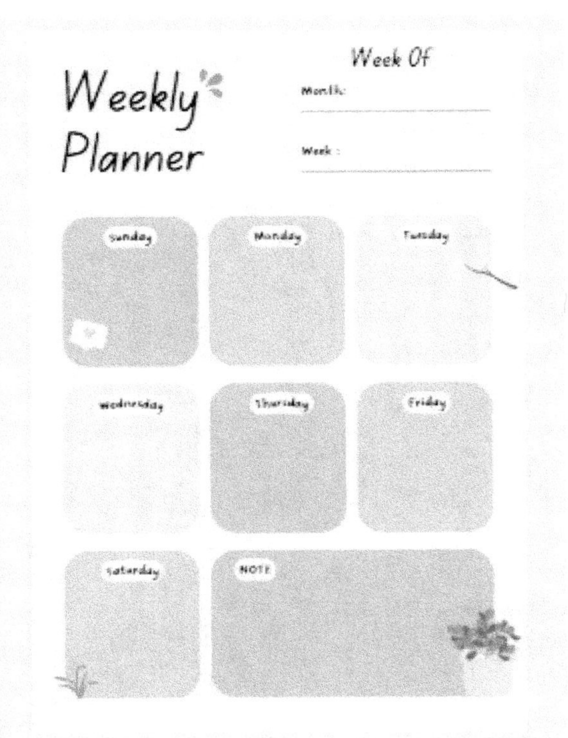

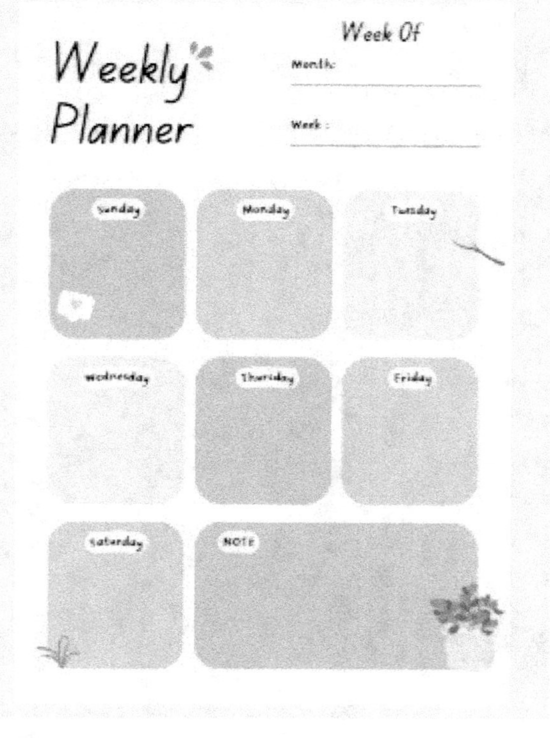

Weekly Planner
Week Of
Month:
Week :
Sunday
Monday
Tuesday
Wednesday
Thursday
Friday
Saturday
NOTE

Weekly Planner
Week Of
Month:
Week :
Sunday
Monday
Tuesday
Wednesday
Thursday
Friday
Saturday
NOTE

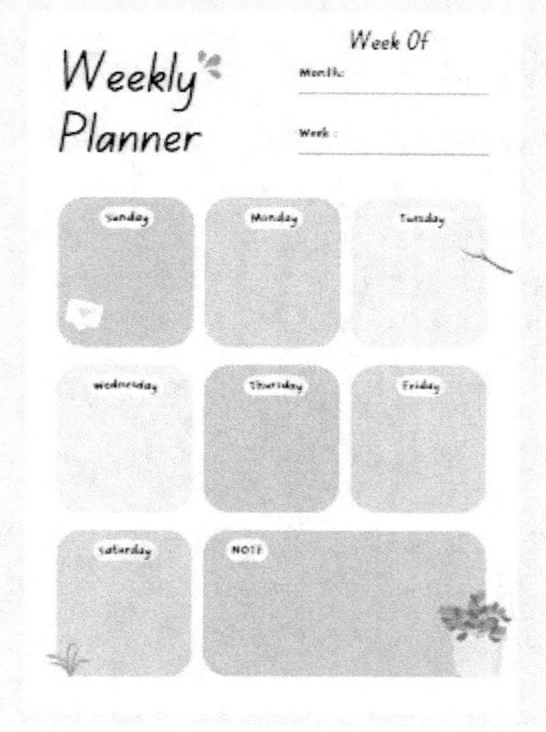

Weekly Planner
Week Of
Month:
Week :
Sunday
Monday
Tuesday
Wednesday
Thursday
Friday
Saturday
NOTE

Weekly Planner
Week Of
Month:
Week :
Sunday
Monday
Tuesday
Wednesday
Thursday
Friday
Saturday
NOTE

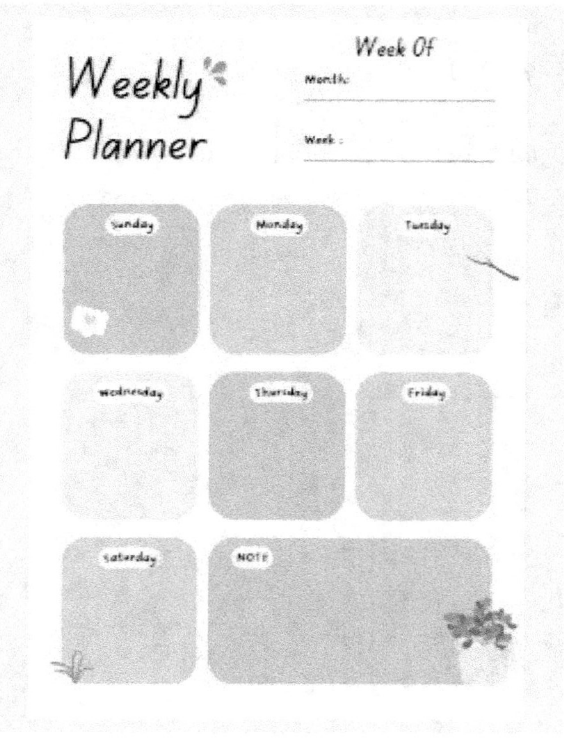

Weekly Planner
Week Of
Month:
Week :
Sunday
Monday
Tuesday
Wednesday
Thursday
Friday
Saturday
NOTE

Weekly Planner
Week Of
Month:
Week :
Sunday
Monday
Tuesday
Wednesday
Thursday
Friday
Saturday
NOTE

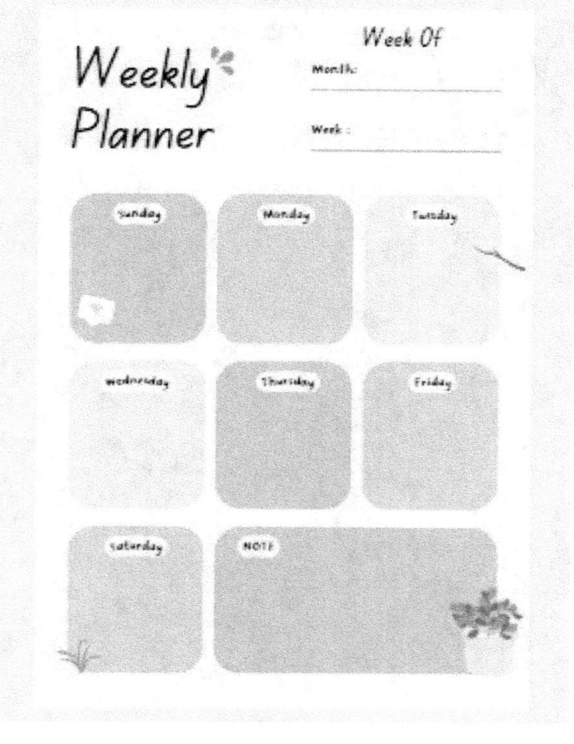

Weekly Planner
Week Of
Month:
Week :
Sunday
Monday
Tuesday
Wednesday
Thursday
Friday
Saturday
NOTE

Extra Weekly Notes

Extra Weekly Notes

Extra Weekly Notes

45

Extra Weekly Notes

Extra Weekly Notes

Extra Weekly Notes

Extra Weekly Notes

Extra Weekly Notes

Extra Weekly Notes

Extra Weekly Notes

Day
Planner
"Everyday lie a memory waiting
to be created"

DATE
M T W T F S S
Scheduled
6 AM
7 AM
8 AM
9 AM
10 AM
11 AM
12 PM
1 PM
2 PM
3 PM
4 PM
5 PM
6 PM
7 PM
8 PM
9 PM
10 PM
11 PM
12 PM

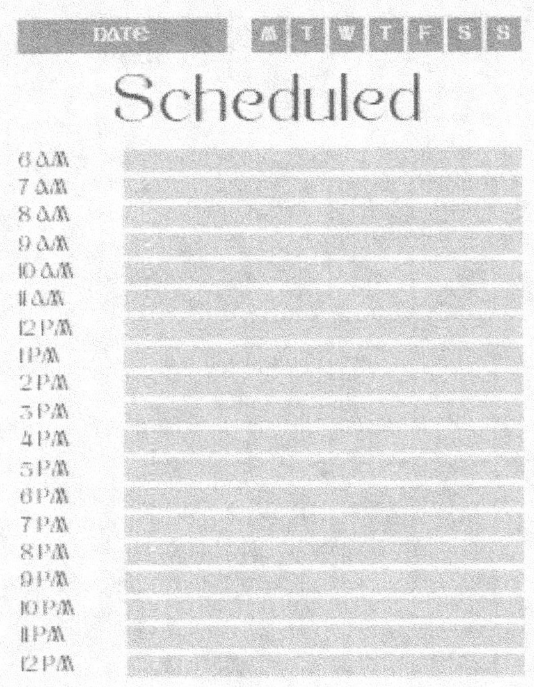

DATE
M T W T F S S
Scheduled
6 AM
7 AM
8 AM
9 AM
10 AM
11 AM
12 PM
1 PM
2 PM
3 PM
4 PM
5 PM
6 PM
7 PM
8 PM
9 PM
10 PM
11 PM
12 PM

DATE
M T W T F S S
Scheduled
6 AM
7 AM
8 AM
9 AM
10 AM
11 AM
12 PM
1 PM
2 PM
3 PM
4 PM
5 PM
6 PM
7 PM
8 PM
9 PM
10 PM
11 PM
12 PM

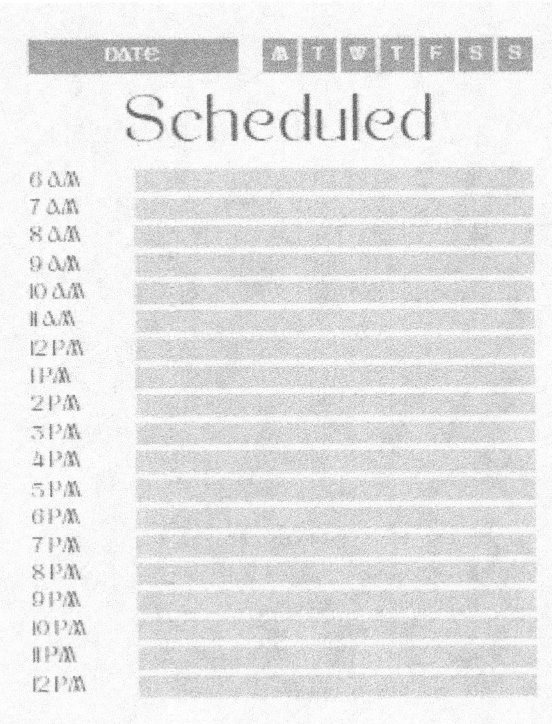

DATE
M T W T F S S
Scheduled
6 AM
7 AM
8 AM
9 AM
10 AM
11 AM
12 PM
1 PM
2 PM
3 PM
4 PM
5 PM
6 PM
7 PM
8 PM
9 PM
10 PM
11 PM
12 PM

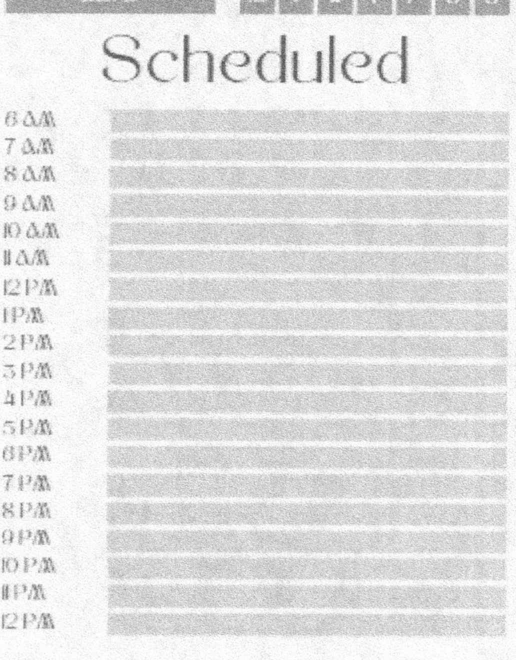

DATE
M T W T F S S
Scheduled
6 AM
7 AM
8 AM
9 AM
10 AM
11 AM
12 PM
1 PM
2 PM
3 PM
4 PM
5 PM
6 PM
7 PM
8 PM
9 PM
10 PM
11 PM
12 PM

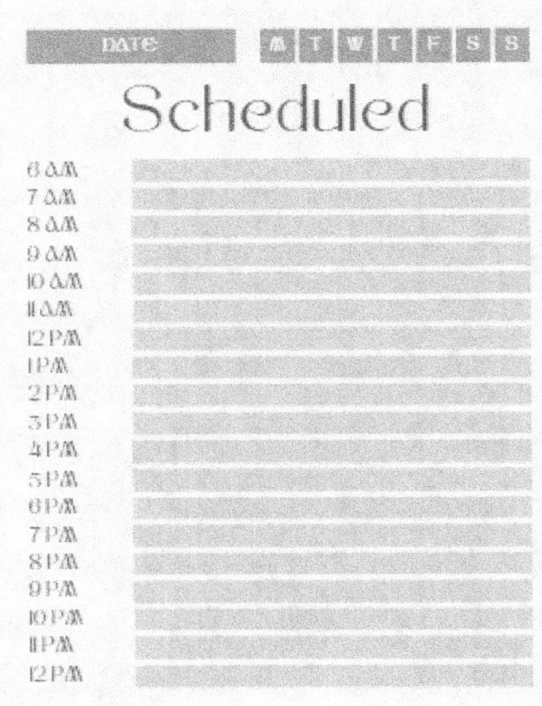

DATE
M T W T F S S
Scheduled
6 AM
7 AM
8 AM
9 AM
10 AM
11 AM
12 PM
1 PM
2 PM
3 PM
4 PM
5 PM
6 PM
7 PM
8 PM
9 PM
10 PM
11 PM
12 PM

DATE
M T W T F S S
Scheduled
6 AM
7 AM
8 AM
9 AM
10 AM
11 AM
12 PM
1 PM
2 PM
3 PM
4 PM
5 PM
6 PM
7 PM
8 PM
9 PM
10 PM
11 PM
12 PM

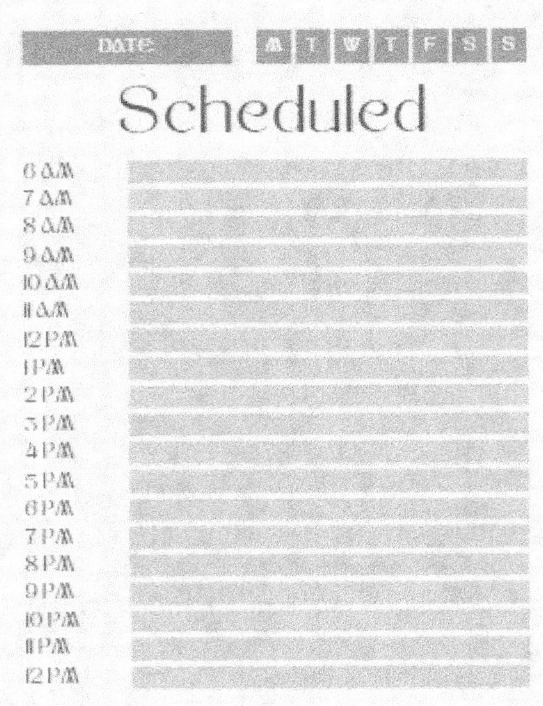

61

DATE:
M T W T F S S
Scheduled
6 AM
7 AM
8 AM
9 AM
10 AM
11 AM
12 PM
1 PM
2 PM
3 PM
4 PM
5 PM
6 PM
7 PM
8 PM
9 PM
10 PM
11 PM
12 PM

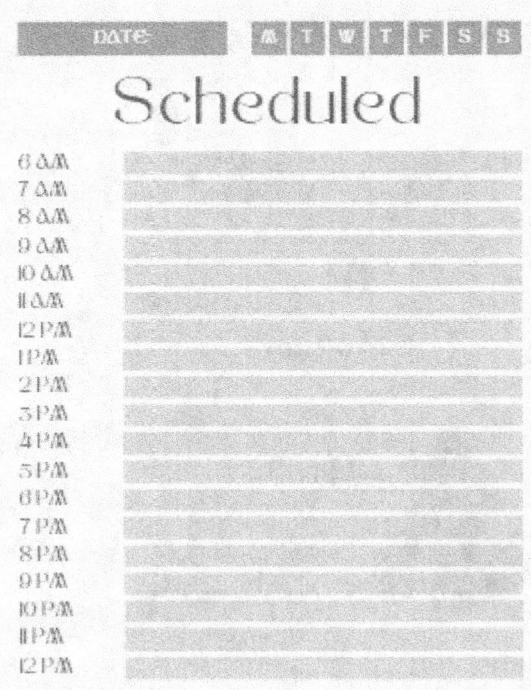

DATE
M T W T F S S
Scheduled
6 AM
7 AM
8 AM
9 AM
10 AM
11 AM
12 PM
1 PM
2 PM
3 PM
4 PM
5 PM
6 PM
7 PM
8 PM
9 PM
10 PM
11 PM
12 PM

Its
The Season
To Be
Jolly

Christmas Gift List

NO	ITEM NAME	QTY	PRICE
1			
2			
3			
4			
5			
6			
7			
8			
9			
10			
11			
12			
13			
14			
15			
TOTAL			

ADDITIONAL NOTES

Christmas Gift List

NO	ITEM NAME	QTY	PRICE
1			
2			
3			
4			
5			
6			
7			
8			
9			
10			
11			
12			
13			
14			
15			
16			
TOTAL			

ADDITIONAL NOTES

Christmas Gift List

NO	ITEM NAME	QTY	PRICE
1			
2			
3			
4			
5			
6			
7			
8			
9			
10			
11			
12			
13			
14			
15			
TOTAL			

ADDITIONAL NOTES

Christmas Gift List

NO	ITEM NAME	QTY	PRICE
1			
2			
3			
4			
5			
6			
7			
8			
9			
10			
11			
12			
13			
14			
15			
16			
TOTAL			

ADDITIONAL NOTES

Christmas Gift List

NO	ITEM NAME	QTY	PRICE
1			
2			
3			
4			
5			
6			
7			
8			
9			
10			
11			
12			
13			
14			
15			
TOTAL			

ADDITIONAL NOTES

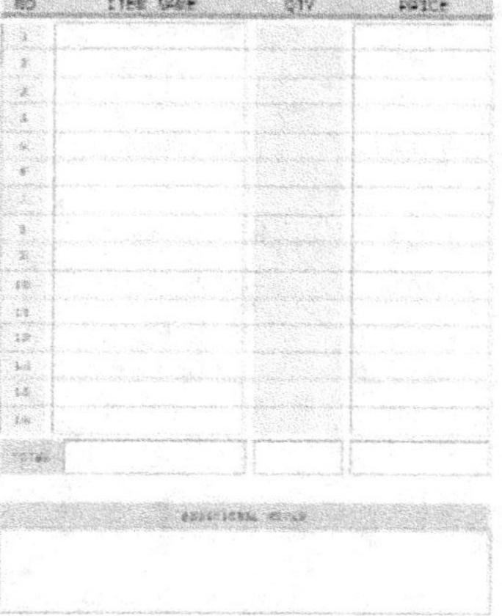
Christmas Gift List
NO   ITEM NAME   QTY   PRICE
TOTAL
ADDITIONAL NOTES

Christmas Gift List

NO	ITEM NAME	QTY	PRICE
1			
2			
3			
4			
5			
6			
7			
8			
9			
10			
11			
12			
13			
14			
TOTAL			

ADDITIONAL NOTES

Christmas Gift List

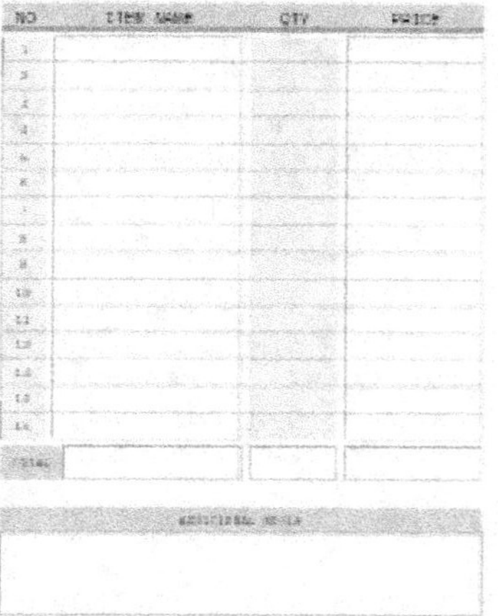

Christmas Gift List

NO.	ITEM NAME	QTY	PRICE
1			
2			
3			
4			
5			
6			
7			
8			
9			
10			
11			
12			
13			
14			
15			
TOTAL			

ADDITIONAL NOTES

Christmas Gift List

Christmas Expense Tracker

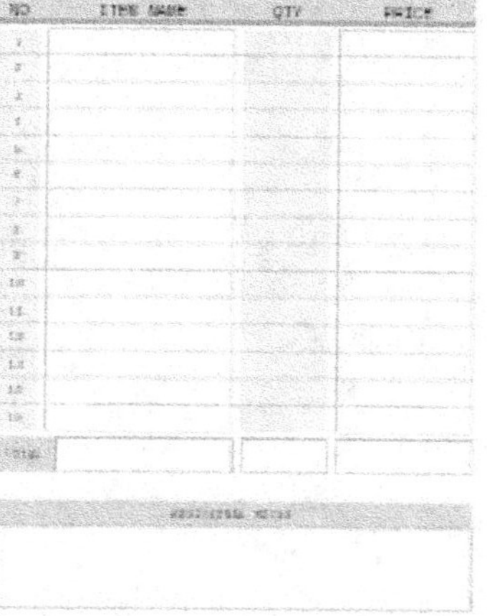

Christmas Expense Tracker

MONTH | YEAR

DATE	AMOUNT	CATEGORY	PLATFORM	NOTES

Christmas Expense Tracker

Christmas Expense Tracker

Christmas Expense Tracker

80

Christmas Expense Tracker

Christmas Expense Tracker

MONTH		YEAR		
DATE	AMOUNT	CATEGORY	OUTCOME	INCOME

Christmas Expense Tracker

MONTH		YEAR		
DATE	AMOUNT	CATEGORY	OUTCOME	INCOME

Christmas Favorite
Recipes
A record for your next Christmas parties!
INGREDIENTS
DIRECTIONS

87

88

Christmas Favorite
Recipes
INGREDIENTS
DIRECTIONS

Christmas Favorite Recipes

INGREDIENTS

DIRECTIONS

Christmas Favorite
Recipes
A record for all your Christmas parties!
INGREDIENTS
DIRECTIONS

92

Christmas Favorite Recipes
Record favorite Christmas recipes!
INGREDIENTS
DIRECTIONS

Christmas Favorite
Recipes

CHIRTMAS MEMORIES

Date :

☐
☐
☐
☐
☐
☐
☐
☐

MY NOTES

96

CHIRTMAS MEMORIES

Date :

MY NOTES

CHIRTMAS MEMORIES
Date :
MY NOTES

CHIRTMAS MEMORIES
Date :
MY NOTES

CHIRTMAS MEMORIES

Date :

☐
☐
☐
☐
☐
☐
☐
☐

MY NOTES

100

CHIRTMAS MEMORIES

Date :

MY NOTES

CHIRTMAS MEMORIES
Date :
MY NOTES

CHIRTMAS MEMORIES

Date :

- [ ]
- [ ]
- [ ]
- [ ]
- [ ]
- [ ]
- [ ]
- [ ]

MY NOTES

New Year Notes

New Year Notes

New Year Notes

New Year Notes

New Year Notes

New Year Notes

New Year Notes

New Year Notes

New Year Notes

New Year Notes

Contents

www.ingramcontent.com/pod-product-compliance
Lightning Source LLC
Chambersburg PA
CBHW081151130726
47996CB00009B/3074

* 9 7 9 8 8 8 8 6 9 5 9 0 6 *